DEAD BOYS IN SPACE

DEAD

Sara

Praise for *DEAD BOYS IN SPACE* by Sara Youngblood Gregory

In this beautiful and inventive project, Sara Youngblood Gregory has reimagined a queer AIDS archive and gifted us with one of the best things queer literature can offer—an alternative story to the dominant narrative—one that imagines us surviving into a future that overlays our grief with defiant, erotic exuberance.
—Keiko Lane, author of *Blood Loss: A Love Story of AIDS, Activism, and Art*

Chilling, whimsical, and endlessly inventive, *DEAD BOYS IN SPACE* utilizes dyke sex as a launching pad into history, an explosion of feeling that radiates in the cosmos of the AIDS crisis. Here Sara Youngblood Gregory provokes a confrontation with societal homophobia that transcends the borders of this planet. By fusing intergenerational grief with embodied imagination, this book offers a new way to mourn.
—Mattilda Bernstein Sycamore, author of *Terry Dactyl*

Sara Youngblood Gregory writes from the generational afterlife of AIDS, where memory is fractured, inherited, and incomplete. The speaker moves through a lingering archive of medical forms that ask about HIV status, political funerals in Tompkins Square Park, the vanished bodies of lovers and brothers, all in search of stories just out of reach and names that were never passed down. These are poems of delight, grief, rumor, conspiracy, and imagination. Some explore a brother who never returns and a government that sends gay men to the moon-histories that feel both distant and devastatingly present. Moving from Southwest Florida's red tides to small-town gay bars, from ACT UP elegies to speculative constellations of the dead, *DEAD BOYS IN SPACE* offers a generational inheritance.
—Steven Reigns, author of *A Quilt for David and Outliving Michael*

BOYS

Youngblood Gregory

SPACE

Cover Art: "Patroclus" © Salomé Grasland, 2025. Used with permission.
Cover and Interior Design: Gatta Olive — Hobbes Ginsberg + Karen Sofia Colón
Project Leads: KMA Sullivan & Karah Kemmerly
Author Photo: Salomé Grasland

ISBN: 978-1-946303-13-4
Printed in the United States of America

Published by YesYes Books
Portland, OR
YesYesBooks.com

I tell you AIDS has really affected my life. You say it's had little or no impact on yours… you say "you're the first person I've ever known with AIDS."

Where the fuck do you live . . . MARS?

W. Wayne Karr, *Infected Faggot Perspectives*, Issue 1, September 1991

CONTENTS

III. DEAD BOYS IN SPACE

IV. SELF PORTRAIT AS SUPER MOON

the only thing you need to know about him is that he's not here

I can't suppose a world in which we meet

(a hero, here, tells me to never meet my heroes)

but I can suppose you

still alive.

Suppose, you, living on Mars.

Going to clubs

on the moon then sleeping over

another man's apartment

but on Mars, or next time Saturn,

where Friday nights are

for breathing diamonds

instead of air.

Suppose

you never get sick.

Suppose there is a rocket that looks like

your crotch

and suppose it takes you to the moon.

There, you party

There, you sleep around

There, our mother doesn't nurse you until you die.

You, nursing a drink.

I do not drink;

I suppose.

Now, here, my greatest leap:

You never heard of AIDS. Mars never existed. You, knowing me,

and your nipples like stars.

Or a mouth.

ANOTHER BODY IN THE SKY

I.

I invent three

The first is the jaybird. Two women passed the color blue between their lips. I realized then women could kiss. I started to choke. The second is a fistful of bird seed. The reason I am promiscuous. I was three, squatting in the woods. I learned to masturbate and when I came so did the birds to the grain. My mother caught me. She said I had a UTI. Then there was the tube inserted in my child-urethra to find out. The third is Salomé's winged vulva.

Climate death but my blood runs hot

the entire coast of southwest Florida chokes herself out red tide
bloats the shore and I strip off my shirt stuff it under the door frame
quick we can smell the dead bodies through every crack the fish
can't breathe and I can't cope their bones are my earrings my dance
card the silver spoon in my mouth mouth the words with me *I love*
you from now until I don't we have always lived like this think AIDS
in the eighties such heat waves of July nineteen eighty-nine my
mother won't tell me if heatstroke killed my brother or the sweating
gorgeous twinks who looked but never found the government still
won't speak our frothy fag names thirty years later they recall how
death equals silence they are killing us and by they I mean capitalists
who blame us and by us I mean the fish the working the broke the
strange the angry the the the the I am almost old before I realize
how silence makes rainstorms out of dykes how every one of our
brothers turned red guts in a glass vase the vice being everything
birds never tell us of ourselves she gasps from between my legs the
only place safe to swim now and her mouth dripping saltwater red
tide fingers and my fish-bone nipples I don't make out the words

Song for my brother

he had a mouth on him his tongue was rough and scratching
flexible those kinds of teeth unusual wide the color blue shallow
what I know about him won't fill cupped hands maybe a bird bath
my missing brother is a migrating bird because gay men never quite
stay each wing is the man I never met but having never met him I
know there's something off about him there is something off about
me if we had met the world would have turned on like chernobyl
packs of radioactive dogs roaming the suburbs of america you just
can't put a reactor too close to the color blue at least not in one
lifetime or in one room ours is the same call us nuclear family

but his mouth

I want to ask who took care of him I want to ask how he died the
name of each lover I imagine the last boy left alive exhausted one
bear sits at a leather bar bare it and grin what did he say about his
own murder? did he live long enough to know he was murdered and
still be dead of it?

I should have tried harder to know you

A medical history form asks, *Have you or a family member ever tested positive for HIV?*

- [ ] Having been told not to open the door, I open the door
- [ ] My mother, cleaning the birdcage
- [ ] Sun-blue, round like a strawberry, small singing
- [ ] The dog rushes the room, and panicking, the bird snaps his neck against the cage
- [ ] Why must every loss take the shape of the first
- [ ] Even now, I recall the feeling of door handles
- [ ] That small turn between guilt and blame

Political funeral

whether we have AIDS or not—whether we are angry or not—whether we are afraid or not—and whether we have a Republican president or not*—a man was there in an open casket in Tompkins Square surrounded by lovers friends accomplices ghosts the eulogy written by a friend who died just before—or not—and this all happened not far from where I live—had not even known—there exists no plaque with the names no statue no stone no plate—just words—mouths—a pundit in place of a person—saying will you eat the ashes or not—yes—then describe the taste of his life—direct action late-night drives empty screen in suits called doctors hand-painted signs survivor's guilt a lover near a window hanging paper cranes on beaded string—or not—my palate only goes so far but what I can picture is the park just this afternoon—children running—loud sounds on the pavement—a paper trail of old men who should be here but aren't—a swing slipping back and forth back and forth and—there—in the middle of it all the opening statement

* Opening lines taken from ACT UP activist Mark Lowe Fisher's eulogy, delivered in 1993. See notes for full quotation.

Eulogy

Thirty years
or more after
your death
my father
mentions you
and each syllable
of your name
is a pearl
spirited
up from some
precious
sinking
grief
my father's
voice
deep-sea
apologetic
or maybe
apologia
I'm not sure
I can hear
the difference
under water
but this is not
how he says
my name
my name
is yellow grain
cracking
as it dries

the shape
of ironed clothes
in the open wind
the chirp
of car doors
locking
and
fathers
teaching
daughters
to dive
listen
there may be
a world
in which
your name
is never
again
spoken
but that
is not
this
world

Gay Related Immune Deficiency (GRID) I

TORCH	SHADE	MOTHER	MOTION
What stands between your legs	Comparing you to a pandemic	Letters not mailed; cursive you were born to	A slot machine every time you have sex
Kissing set to "Rocket Man"	Sodomites saying family	The way I am still inside her when you die	How I would kill to be only 6 feet from you
Antonyms; symptoms; anatomy	3 feet by 6	Long shadows where she kneels on a perfect day	Control; crowds condoms
Me, looking back	Duane Kearns Puryear, 1987	You, not waiting	A coin sliding into its notch

Come and see the place where he lay

I call you tide-bringer

I call you birds-diving

I call you keeper

shame-stealer

stampede

he-has-risen

I call you Cain

I call you sight-of-God

I call you memory

I call you mine

Constellation

Why does your life feel like a trail. Or maybe a comet. I saw one once. A comet, a real one. The size of a penny held close enough to your eye, but in the sky instead of your hand. Shiny, with long hair down its back. I felt alive and my eyes hurt. Earlier that day I drove five hours to the knock-off NASA museum, convinced I would crash and die the entire ride. I was dizzy, too, in my supposing. I didn't even know the comet was coming. Still, I cried at the museum, looking at all that glossy-thick plastic. The roped-off dust. The empty helmets. My fingers itched, looking at those screens and panels and tubes. It was almost *medical*.

Oh. The comet. Did you see it, too. When I was there, later that night, crouched in a motel parking lot, squinting and watching and breathing. It was primal and humid. There was broken glass. It flashed blue with headlights. The moon was not in the sky, I realized. When did you last see the moon. I usually get distracted. Rushing here or there.

Was our mother's womb like another planet for you, too. Was it distracting. Or just another body in the sky. Did you know it was me yet. Because I was there, floating in that dusky space, tethered by a woman. I imagine your hand on me. Like God. Rock-solid and whispering. I think about you sometimes, living in the sky. I stay awake at night aching for you, that slow leak of poison. Do you drift off sometimes, sleeping in that dark and wet. Do you drift literally. From lack of gravity, I mean.

I imagine myself as the wife of Lot sometimes, salty and bitter and burning for you, your exile, which I can witness but never stop. I rarely wear red. What color are your eyes. And do you remember our mother. Do you remember the sound of our father growing up. I love them. Their silence is long. Did you ever listen for me. What happens if you never come home?

Ghost

The question is not why my brother had to die.

The question is how do I save him.

SHOOT THE QUEERS

II.

BLOODSHIFT

TAKE A HANDFUL OF SWAMP AND —————— WAIT

————————————————————

———————————— WADE ——————————

———————————— FEEL THE MUD BROWN AND

—— DROWNING ——————————————

——————————————— MAKE A ——————

—————————— FIST ——————————

————————————————————

—————————————————— BLOODSHIFT

———————————— SLIPSTREAMS AND ————

—— WET DREAMS ———————————

————————————————————

————————————————————

————————————— I'M CLEARING MY THROAT

————————————————————

YOU'RE HOLDING ————————————

————————————————————

—————————— MY NECK ——————————

MY WRIST YOUR BROKEN

HANDS

THE TANNINS IN THE

WATER

THE GAS MASK

THE PORCELAIN

THINGS ARE ABOUT TO GO

VERY QUICKLY

YOU WARM ME

WOMEN DROWNING

WOMEN

SUB

MISSIVE

SUB

MARINE

MY DOMME IS FULLY

CLOTHED

AT THE LIP

OF THE TUB

SOVIET LATEX GP-5 WITH HOSE

(GOOGLE IF CONFUSED)

THE FEMME IS WEARING THE
MASK

THE FEMME IS ALWAYS WEARING
THE MASK
SWEARING

YOUR HANDS
MAKE A
PRAYER

TAP FROM THE
INSIDE
SLIDE

LIKE A FISH BOWL

MICROPHONE

MOAN

WHAT IT IS TO BE HUMAN CHANGES

UNDER WATER

WHAT IT IS

YOU

FISTING

ME

WITH A

FIST

FULL

OF

GOD

WHAT IS IT

____

____

——————— GET BORN AGAIN ———————

____

——— BRADYCARDIA —— IN A NORTH FLORIDA ———

____

——————————————— TUB ——————

____

————————————— FUCKING IS ——————

____

____

———————— BUT ——————————

——— DROWNING ——————————

____

—————————————— IS FETAL ——————

____

FULL ——————————————————

METAL —————————————————

____

————————————— THE TENSION ——————

——————————— BETWEEN ——————————

SURFACE

AND

AMBIENT

ORGASM REFUSING

RELEASE

RELIEF

I'D RATHER

SEARCH

SURGE

BOTTLENECK THAT TURN

WE DON'T CARE ABOUT CUMMING

TONGUING

OR RUNNING

WATER

ALL WE CARE ABOUT IS

AND FLOODING THE FUCKING WORLD

Planet the shape of a fist

No one tricked anyone. The dance
was fair and square and I begged
her for it. Each dip and thrust, the
slight of wrist, the chorus of justice.
Justice? Yes. Don't be a sore loser.
The scales are tipping ever away.
Think blood made of rhythm, lust lock-
step with loss, revenge on a short leash.
Anger is a blade you must grasp firmly,
she tells me. Otherwise history slips
through and away, makes a wound
nothing but a wound. How could I not
love her—my body a knife, her hands
the hilt? And the seven veils which were never
veils, but bandages sewn from our dead.
I want this world on a platter, Salomé.

There is nothing immortal about getting even

I lay outside your altar

it's the second truly hot day of spring

the quilt beneath is covered in prayers

and names so dirty and soft

I resist the urge to suck my thumb

while burning a hospital to the ground

look at me

you are the only girl in the Bible

who ever got away with anything

I am the fanatic at your feet

let me bind your chest tighter, closer

let me shave your head against the grain

can you smell the gasoline?

one does not burn without the other

which is how we like it

Cardinal

elaine scarry writes, *for the person in pain, so incontestably and unnegotiably present is it that 'having pain' may come to be thought of as the most vibrant example of what it is to 'have certainty,' while for the other person it is so elusive that 'hearing about pain' may exist as the primary model of what it is 'to have doubt'* /

salomé says anyone with a marginalized identity / let's call them cardinals / any cardinal at all / lives her life tense under threat / her body seals up that tension because she expects a fight / her whole life is a fight / her wings are brittle from hugging her own body from snapping out too quick / the egg inside has never slept through the night / whatever tension from her mother's womb and her mother's mother's womb is now the cardinal's womb / cardinals don't mean to carry it / it is forced / structural generational carnal a carnival / the womb is different from ovaries / or eggs / or anything certain / the womb is the body she sleeps in / the primary model of what it is to have doubt / look / there is a window in my ankle bone / kneel down / put your eye to my body / your lips to my calf she is atrophied / look closer / and there again is the anger of patroclus /

he is wandering my body / he is tragedy / stray arrow straight shot stray burial / Patroclus takes up the mantle or doesn't / you tell me / I can't see inside my own womb I only feel / shovel striking dirt /

amy berkowitz writes, *in 1970, a german activist group called the socialist patients' collective recognized capitalism as the root cause of all illness. to be sick, then, was a political act: a passive resistance against capitalism. the group's slogan: turn illness into a weapon.* /

Vertigo

ten days before I am disowned my head spins three days after I am disowned (my mother on the phone screaming I am sick) I am sick & the world (sick) starts to spin again, but faster again, but full time

it's the crystals in my ears it was the road trip the mountains the badlands the arizona desert that goddamn fire that plane to new york the altitudes or all three fill up ear canals full of fluid the ocean & mother's wet, young blood (how dare you write that) straight to my brain & suffocate

crystals in my head decide when earth is flat when we (you, me, mother, think how this affects us) walk straight crystal four & final is gravity like a compass the only one not in my head spins 'til I am sick sick all over some dress and frills I sink to the surface grasp, puke, rip off lace (all you ever do is run away)

Gay Related Immune Deficiency (GRID) II

WATER	MIRROR	WINDOW	APOLOGY
Sappho's first kiss	Me, staring at the songbird staring back	Magic 8 ball, top drawer	You never said stop—
Mouth; tongue; dive	You wouldn't even have a book if it weren't for—	The way I am still inside her when you die	I did
Leucadian cliff	You'd be dead if I hadn't—	Can you stop looking out the window and just—	You didn't mean to—
Concentrate and ask again	Healthcare; silence; cloth over a cage	Water under certain lighting	I did

How to be a wormhole

Cut your hair / Feel sick / Sicker than you have ever been / Talk / Talk again / Ask who's new in town / Tell them where they went wrong / Remind them how you would have done it better / Never brag / Look ugly / Exude lust when you walk through the ankle / Of a star / Then / Excuse it / Lie when easy / The truth becomes no one / But hard things become you / Name your cats / Anger and Altruism / Which sleep at your feet / Eat fingers like carrots / Suck cars through a straw / Grow / Grow so heavy the spine of light bends back on itself / Then snaps / Puke up the bones / Leave dirt in your house / Leave planets wrinkled in corners / Squish ecosystems / Fish around the jar for bubble gum / Pop / Then spit / That was a cherry-flavored moon / Not your favorite / Drink helium until you speak in gasps / It carries like explosion / Let your head hit the ceiling / Of what? / Trip over history / Which for you is a Sunday / Laugh at the scabs / Pick them and watch streets panic in your blood / Cut your hair / The universe is a split end

The same outline that proves he was here is the same that proves he is gone

It would be a palm

pressed into the pavement of a sidewalk,

next to initials and a year.

There would be the handprint

and the uneven splotches of cement,

the disrupted level

marking where a finger dragged

across the wet and pressed surely

into the path of my life.

Tell me,

if I have never seen the hand

but for its lack with what else

can it be filled but temper

but lust but the backwater

taste of his full name

in my open mouth.

Salomé / Dark Blue

1

My girlfriend and my girlfriend kiss second hand
from her lips to my lips to her lips to mine
then the other to mine then back then restart.
If you can't imagine what I do
with my girlfriend and my girlfriend
that's the point.

2

My lovers gather in the temple.
Salomé's pussy turns explosion.
The smell of fish frying.

3

I break up with my girlfriend and
I stay with my girlfriend. Perverts in the water,
pyros in the sea. There are more women
than my girlfriend and my former girlfriend.
The way we manage to share one mouth.

4

I show up late to the underwater temple.

My lovers there are ugly. I am there ugly.

The knife slips through the bucket.

The knife guts the fish. Guts explode the world.

What is ugly defiles.

5

I don't compare myself to Salomé

when Salomé has a cock. Whose clothes

make my bed? Whose teeth my mouth?

On the end of the line, dark blue.

There is heavy breathing. Am I still

angry?

6

The cock is the mangrove snake. The mouth

is the mouth. The body is never the temple.

7

My girlfriend and my former girlfriend.

Me and my lovers the uglies. We are climbing

the trees. From up in the trees the uglies look

down. We show up early and kill what doesn't suit.

8

On the shoreline there is a snake for every mouth.

There is a bucket for every hole. The second hand

the knife the explosion Salomé still angry

and the smell of what this time doesn't get away.

It used to be illegal for homosexuals to rest like this

I'm lying in bed with my girlfriend and a kitten shaking in my hands suckles on my finger they both do out loud I read David Wojnarowicz from shortly before his death he says every T-cell lost is ten pounds of rage gained but he is so skinny from sick and so fat with raging I think he must be a god I can see him in my mind's eye see him in the eyes of a kitten of a dyke lover in bed next to me sticky with sleep the children of AIDS are connected by blood infection & sneaking out windows never to be seen again we are our parents' bastards of a disease that is still killing us and my god I miss the elders I have never known

"if you want to stop AIDS, shoot the queers" says the Texas governor ten years before I was born a curse laid on my life I scroll on my phone and read this time "abortion hope after 'gay genes' finding" am I an overgrown abortion & what if I prefer that?

David's fantasy is a clotted baby slipping through back doors and crawling face-first wild on the streets suckling ten pounds of raging one year at a time it's simple *if you want to stop AIDS, shoot the queers*

my open hands are an open target and did you see the news lately?
all bathroom bills and bedroom bans? or how the cost of PrEP
makes us laugh? the only thing queer that hasn't gone pop

(imagine here the long sharp teeth of gorgeous women who
will never pass)

is our raging my lover still in bed next to me saying *I'm trying to sleep* went to therapy for the rage I mentioned and the therapist said *I won't change my mind about homosexuals if you are only 10 percent of the population* meaning there is still hope for abortion late-term self-performed & remember when David was alive? how his raging was so big and we were everywhere? how in '85 we were still half the universe?

DEAD BOYS IN SPACE

III.

One Million Dead Men: An Empirical Investigation Into New Sodom

October, Year 2577
Center for the Study of the
National Aeronautics and Space Administration
Transcripts courtesy of CS-NASA

PROFESSOR: Thank you for joining me this evening. First and foremost, I must thank our generous HOST for sponsoring this lecture and for allowing me a bit of secrecy around today's agenda. After many years of study and many months of planning, I am thrilled to finally share the results of my research this evening with such esteemed scholars, patrons, and most importantly, officials of State and Force. The topic at hand is actually one we all know about—or rather one we *think* we know about—the space colonization of the twentieth and twenty-first centuries.

[THE CROWD MURMURS]

PROFESSOR: Now, you have all been briefed before your arrival, but I will go over the more fundamental aspects of this colonization—that which even a child would likely know—and begin complicating this story, layer by layer. My aim, friends, is to separate the parable from the plausible.

Now, please direct your attention to the screen behind me.

– – –

SLIDE ONE: GAY MEN ON THE MOON, SENT BY THE UNITED STATES GOVERNMENT FOR THEIR UNIQUE BIOLOGICAL AND SOCIO-CULTURAL MERIT.

– – –

PROFESSOR: An estimated 1.6 million homosexual men aged 24 to 44 were successfully displaced and relocated to the Lunar Base between 1981 and 1996.

Though you may have learned that *all* homosexuals were relocated, this idea is a latent, yet potent, remnant of the government's disinformation campaign of the late twentieth and early twenty-first centuries. See how myth can fly?

So, what happened to the very young? The very old?

Efforts were made to relocate elderly homosexual men, many of whom were previously cataloged, within a small margin of error, during the so-called Red Scare of the 1950s. However, these men died too quickly for systematic accounting or rehoming.

And unlike this older population, which was more likely to be known and surveilled, homosexual men *under* 24 often lacked the necessary intergenerational mentorships and subcultural spaces needed to enact their sexuality. As mass raids of neighborhoods, bars, and bedrooms became increasingly frequent and ever more granular, many in the sub-24 population chose celibacy in order to avoid the attention of so-called body snatchers. How, then, would one identify every boy with a homosexual thought? It's sifting sand with sand—impossible.

However, 85 percent of all those diagnosed with AIDS throughout the epidemic were between 20 and 49. In other words, the lunar colonization did *effectively* wipe out the entire homosexual male population in the United States, even if there is more nuance than popular history allows. Moving on now . . .

— — —

SLIDE TWO: THE COLONIZATION EFFORT WAS TWOFOLD: TO SAFEGUARD THE REST OF THE UNITED STATES FROM WHAT WAS THEN CALLED HIV-AIDS, AND TO CLAIM THE REST OF THE SOLAR SYSTEM AS AMERICAN SOIL.

— — —

PROFESSOR: The Cold War began in 1947, though in reality this conflict was more a hotbed of violence than a permafrost.

Uprisings, proxy wars, psychological assault, iron curtains, red red borders, chemicals, nuclear armies . . . no single speaker, no single presentation, no solitary man could ever begin to pull at that thread of conflict. No. Our focus, then, must be only the Space Race.

The true turning point began with the Sputnik crisis of '57. The USSR launched the first successful satellite, Sputnik I, into space—a humiliation for the United States government and a fraying of confidence for its people.

Power, you see, isn't who holds the knife. It's making sure you are never found empty-handed. Or so thought our ancestors.

Four years later, Yuri Gargarin—young, whip-thin, a dedicated communist—became the first human ever to enter outer space in the Vostok I. This craft was not overly impressive, as it resembled a cramped, over-heavy fishbowl. Yet you can imagine how alien defeat must have seemed to Yuri's enemies.

On May 25, 1961, the United States president—part figurehead, part commander, part empty screen—asked his country to pledge to "landing a man on the moon and returning him safely to the Earth" before the decade was out. The country rallied to the cause.

This was the point of no return.

— — —

SLIDE THREE CONTAINS SIDE-BY-SIDE IMAGES. ON THE RIGHT, THE BARREN LUNAR SURFACE BEFORE COLONIZATION. ON THE LEFT, THE SURFACE IS CROWDED WITH DARK BUILDINGS, CLEAN GLASS, A BARE FLAGPOLE.

IN 1998, US MILITARY OFFICIALS FINALLY CONCEDED THAT THE LUNAR COLONIZATION MISSION FAILED.

— — —

PROFESSOR: Imagine the audacity of such a plan. The genius! I can think of no better strategy to form and perfect a fully functional, life-sustaining Moon Colony than through the deployment of a population with an expiration date and no possibility of procreation. A population who, given enough time and resources, will fuck themselves to death.

[A VOICE FROM THE CROWD: THEY DIDN'T WANT TO GO, DID THEY?]

HOST: Please hold all questions until the presentation is over.

— — —

PROFESSOR: Thank you, HOST. Now, as I was saying . . .

The AIDS epidemic coincided quite fatefully with the Space

Race. Colliding with nationalism, the American obsession with the frontier, as well as advances in technology, medicine, and fanaticism, these two seemingly disparate crises became locked in twin orbit, all the while spinning faster and faster and out of control.

The first man—mark me, a real astronaut, *not* a homosexual—landed on the moon in 1969, making good on the president's extracted promise.

The first known record of HIV-AIDS from a governmental agency was 12 years later in 1981. First referred to as Gay-Related Immune Deficiency, or GRID, the Centers for Disease Control published a small report about an unusual lung infection afflicting five gay men in the then-populous city of Los Angeles. However, some sources suggest anecdotal word-of-mouth reports of a strange illness had spread amongst the community, even in the form of local radio wave broadcasts, as early as 1978. There's an old expression—*canary in a coal mine*.

Regardless, by 1981 the epidemic was burning through boys left and right, the Cold War was nuke-hot, and the flag on the moon was getting lonely.

The project was announced publicly after 25 percent of men with a confirmed diagnosis were permanently resettled on the Moon Colony via Patroclus flights 10 through 200. The President showed grainy, but distinct, photos of the gay men living on the colony in compound structures. This was during the State of the Union address in '85. That is nineteen hundred and eighty-five, yes. Seems like a long time ago, doesn't it? Well, it isn't.

From a scientific perspective, this was a landmark achievement. A fact beyond reproach.

However, in my research I found that much of the global population at the time believed the growing Lunar Base was fake. Other nations took it as a wholesale sign of desperation that the US would use such bizarre propaganda methods—and consequently, those nations began to move more boldly against American empire on Earth.

Ironically, the colony meant to settle the Cold War once and for all actually lit the match.

[NOISES FROM THE CROWD]

PROFESSOR: Within a year of the colony's collapse, the Soviets flew some sort of small dog to the moon, strapped with cameras to investigate, leading to the eventual exchange of nuclear arms between the two nations. The dog's name was Lucky. This will be important later.

Now, to answer the query from the crowd. The homosexual community was overwhelmingly supportive of leaving Earth. And given what became of those left Earth-bound, this exiled population showed, from what I understand, uncharacteristic foresight by embracing space travel.

Though of course, there is some discussion as to the *extent* of that willingness on an individual level. Most boys gladly left their families, jobs, homes, planet . . . But there are some fringe testimonials from Earth-bound families who protested the raids, the surveillance, the separation from loved ones . . . there are scattered reports of riots of undetermined size . . . even some limited records of human rights complaints and/or violations.

But naturally, these alleged concerns fall outside the scope of my research.

– – –

PROFESSOR: Now, before communication from the moon was completely cut off in '96, we do know that there were functioning nightclubs, saunas, and workstations—including greenhouses, mechanics, air quality assurance, reclamation centers that recycled water from urine, feces, sweat, and, yes, semen.

But

There was a problem.

The men weren't dying.

Of the odd few million men who lived, worked, breathed, and slept on the moon, none were reported dead in the first five years of transmissions.

There are two popular explanations we were all taught. First, some claim with certainty that a prolonged state in low gravity suspended the effects of HIV, even AIDS. This is simply fanciful thinking, not science.

Others theorize that fifth column insurgents hacked into the main computers and turned off the Death Count System—a sort of symbolic yet maddening protest against the government's response to AIDS. Further supporting this theory were the similarities with

Earth-bound "die-in protests" popular amongst radicalized female homosexual and transsexual factions.

The Death Count System mattered to the politicians back home. It acted as a sort of timer, ticking lower and lower with each death in the population. When the number hit zero, the Lunar Base would be ready for its true occupants. The gateway to the stars would open. A return on investment in sight.

While this theory is certainly thrilling—hackers, protests, and angry presidents—it's impossible. On the moon, death was tied up in every decision, every bit of data—how many times a toilet was flushed, a bed slept in, a tap turned on, a piece of fruit consumed. No, there was no way anyone could have duped the Death Count System.

These men were simply . . . alive.

[THE SOUND OF A BIRD,

SCREECHING]

[TALONS VIA BLUETOOTH]

HOST: Please settle down. You will be removed from this chamber if you disturb the presentation. All your questions will be answered.

May the officers address the intruders . . . and please pick up that woman off the floor. I believe she passed out. Is she shaking? A medic maybe as well . . . No? Just leave her there for now.

[SOUNDS OF CHAIRS SCRAPING THE FLOOR,
LOW CURSING, CONFUSION]

[THE BIRDS ARE CAUGHT, ESCORTED AWAY]

HOST: Please, professor, continue . . .

— — —

PROFESSOR: It's hard to imagine what AIDS was like. The oldest among us, even generations removed, could not remember a time when AIDS was actually Earth-bound. It simply does not exist here. In this, the colonization was successful.

I have read reports, real medical reports, from doctors during the time predating colonization.

Imagine a half-man.

A skeleton, walking around, struggling to keep skin slipping from the shoulder. Trays of food left outside hospital rooms, nurses too hateful to cross doorways, men too starved to bend down. Mothers feeding sons in childhood bedrooms, lovers touching hunger, holding hands.

PICTURE IT.

LET IT BE SEARED INTO YOU.

LET YOU NOT LOOK AWAY.

PROFESSOR: Somehow,

and alone but for each other, these exiles put a stopper on one of the most aggressive illnesses in the history of mankind . . . once they touched down on the lunar surface, not a single gay man died of AIDS.

Then, for some unknown reason, they *decided* to die together, all at once, in a single day.

This is what we were told, that long-ago myth spread by American officials: the men died via mass suicide.

But Why?

upon realizing they would not die of

AIDS,

did they decide to die anyway?

The official history does not make sense.

Why would these men abandon so quickly what seemed to be a functional Eden with all the benefits of Sodom?

If they were so seemingly untouchable by either God, death, or country . . .

what did they know that we don't?

In order to answer this query, I gained entry to the restricted archives from Geneva, which were never digitized and instead stored in an underground bunker in Fallout Zone 28. From transcripts discussing Lucky's voyage in 1999, I know that there were no dead bodies to be found on the Moon Colony. The greenhouses were overgrown jungles. The showers were still hot, the saunas still steaming.

The morgues were empty and the water ran clear.

The beds were made, but rooms were stripped of personal possessions—photos of family members, love letters, condoms, electric fans, blankets, clothing, all missing. And of course, the rockets (which, one scientist noted after the final Patroclus flight, "littered the moon's surface like headstones")?

All of them gone.

– – –

PROFESSOR: Esteemed scholars, patrons, officials of State and Force . . . what I am about to disclose is considered heresy.

THESE MEN ARE NOT D—

[A SINGLE SHOT RINGS OUT]

[A BODY FALLING TO THE FLOOR]

[CRYING OR PERHAPS LAUGHTER]

– – –

THE SOUND OF A THOUSAND WINGS

AND

THE UNIVERSE ABOVE

TURNING,

TURNING

SELF PORTRAIT AS SUPER MOON

IV.

Blood Sister / Only Child

I keep your history
the one you never asked for
and which outlines my grief but never yours

You don't belong in scripture
        or legends or congratulatory myth
A story isn't enough and neither is sorry

But when I don't know what to say
        I say *sorry*
I say *this time I will tell it right*

To make you real I needed what was real
        microchips and screens, jet engines and rats
in small cages injected with other small cages

In writing an elegy I accidentally discovered
        conspiracy and its opposite
the short, red clay music of dirge
                played by a computer

The entire night sky is your wake
        because the entire night sky is your body

I, that strange keeper, keep you there
so one more person can look down on me
Look down on me

For all this time I spent in anger
I should have known
only women may lead the keening wail

        which in the end is just another dance
                one part breast, one part poem,
and then just one

The center of the universe is a small-town gay bar

The bar was packed on a Wednesday and the line stretched down the road I was wearing tights for winter it was snowing outside inside I was sweating through the nylon and the black of my dress which dykes and old queens dolls and young young men were hitching up as they slipped past I didn't mind there were so many waists and hands and fabrics they all blend together except for when I felt someone new press by in slacks there was water beading on her shoulders like a birthmark her chest was bound and her hair was short and she didn't touch my hem which is how I knew she wanted to and how I knew she was for me I followed her and the music tangled up with my voice it was so loud we didn't speak we danced I was pushy and she pushed back and then we found our rhythm she snapped my damp tights between her thumb and forefinger and I laughed which sounded like nothing over the music or maybe like I opened my mouth and became music I read her lips and she said *you have the smallest teeth I've ever seen* which is not a compliment exactly but something that instead says *I am looking at you hard* which is all that matters when the music is so good and the lights follow no particular patterns except when she dips her lips down to meet mine *what's your name* I say but already know later she will remind me how I loved her first but for now it is enough to sweat into each other's mouths surrounded on all sides by strangers and the coming day

If you ask me why I read science fiction

The answer is that there is no such thing

as fiction

there are just worlds

as bad as this one

yes

but different

worlds with hellfire

the shape of trees

places with no stars   no women

no squares of sunlight

resting on thick carpet

for a yellow cat

because carpets do not exist there

and the sun is just a narrow hole

which people underneath worship

in worlds

not unlike this one

but

in different worlds

there is singing

and praise

spread out

like dandelion fluff

which

in some versions of the past

are edible

and used for money

places

even

where skyscrapers are portals

and birds pass through

unharmed

where girls with veiled faces slink

through the eye of a needle

as easily

as a doorway

worlds

where open air markets have hallways

and there is no such word as

lonely or *lost*

and

as a result

we run into each other

and marvel

how lucky

of you

to be

where you are

and the odds

of

me

being here

where

I am

with

you

Gay Related Immune Deficiency (GRID) III

BIRD	DYKE	PAIN	APOLOGY
My HIV status; yours	Water- stopping dams	Ruby- throated daughter	I thought you wanted—
Oscar Wilde's *Salomé*	Window; mouth; blade	Ghost limb; hysteria; dark blue	I do
Morgue the shape of a box	The choice between bathrooms	Any word that rhymes with *have* *you heard* *of ACT UP?*	Apology
Butterflies; brothers; I miss you	Translation of *sputnik*	The razing of Institut für Sexualwiss- enschaft, 1933	I love you

As Super Moon

Opposition in the night sky

Opposition in the way Salomé handles my hand

I write about it for work:
hate crimes like stars
laws like a blade
and
Jupiter
luster-dark, bigger than an apple,
red where you touch me

sweeps toward earth, its closest trajectory in decades
opposite of home, but better

What is also a super moon:
how when I started writing this I was in love
how I settle in a field starved well enough from light
how I don't need eyes to see birds,

but keep them

anyway

He's there, in the sky, not squinting back

He's got a new apartment now
a new boyfriend or two
rocket fuel for lube

He's happy

younger than me now

when did that happen?

gestures from the red giant

Please, I say,

tell me what to do

Though they thought we were caged, we were actually sewing

The grid is the curse

The grid is the cage

The grid is the exact

width

of your

blood

NO

He says to me, finally, finally

Look back and again

Slowly, now

Look

And Remember:

History is not the blade History is the woman

the pillar of salt

And the gaze that does not burn

but spins over and over

wider and

wider

like the cool blue light

of a star

lapping in our hands

Speak

And Remember:

anything you contain, you exile

And they cannot contain us all

Look! He says

the grid is actually the quilt

O and the wind truly does catch

The AIDS Memorial Quilt is the largest community art project in the universe. First conceived in 1985, the AIDS Quilt honors and celebrates the lives of those lost to AIDS. There are over 50,000 panels, all 3 feet by 6, or the size of a standard grave. Despite this, the quilt is not a funeral shroud.

Each square of fabric is blue deep deep hungry blue no matter what color you see on the square just know its true color is blue blue passing back and forth into light slipping past electricity the physics of explanation or divination this type of blue upends shades or shadow or dying like a river tilting against the swollen ripe of a solar eclipse which, together, sends millions of crescents darting across water except now there are a million and a million slices of blue like an ocean gushing forth from the dimensions of a mathematical grid the square footage of a single grave—impossible only if you fight it—the patterns multiply of their own accord they follow no tide just flow in fat droplets of blue imagine one million, two million, three then infinite sets of hands, sometimes four or five to a single body, raising the AIDS Quilt at the same time and then imagine the weight of all those lives, the self-portraits the ghosts and grief and parties and glory—54 tons and counting—and it's all light as a feather like children thrusting a polka dot parachute upward on a bright day then rushing under it all at once to sit and breathe the same air except everything is blue and the hands do not go under the cloth but rise and the quilt is a sail catching in the wind O and the wind truly does catch lifting higher and higher a parachute that goes up, eternally, and never down can you see them all spinning, holding on to the quilt but not needing to because now there are millions and millions of birds sometimes two, four, six to a body can you hear them laughing at the perversity of a winged carousel the color of the sky or water or mirrors or kissing and, actually, the rest of us are just lucky to have witnessed the launch the G force of which makes it so they are still spinning spinning slowly spinning spinning into the mouth of the universe swallow spin spit wave your hand wave your hand again say *wanderer*, say *good-bye*, say *tell me when you get home safe!*

Notes

1. "I invent three" borrows its title from the opening line of sam sax's poem "Psychotherapy," published in their 2017 collection *Madness*.

2. The opening lines of "Political funeral" are taken from a series of eulogies published in Sarah Schulman's *Let the Record Show: A Political History of ACT UP New York 1987–1993*. As Schulman describes, the eulogy was written by Jon Greenberg for his friend Mark Lowe Fisher. When Greenberg died—having been unable to read Fisher's eulogy himself—Barbara Hughes read it at Greenberg's own funeral at Tompkins Square Park in New York City on July 16, 1993. Unlike some other political funerals of the time, it was open casket. Inside, Greenberg was dressed in drag and, later, as instructed, some friends would eat his ashes.

   The full quotation reads: "Mark has once again crossed a boundary that each of us will sooner or later have to cross, whether we have AIDS or not, whether we are angry or not, whether we are afraid or not, and whether we have a Republican president or not. The truth is that each of us will one day follow Mark to that ultimate otherness and the final liberation."

3. All three GRID poems borrow a modified form of Franny Choi's poem "Glossary of Terms," published in her 2019 collection *Soft Science*.

4. "Come and see the place where he lay" is from Matthew 28:6. But the form and language of this poem closely mirrors Judy Grahn's poem "Paris and Helen," from *love belongs to those who do the feeling: New & Selected Poems (1966–2006)*.

5. "Cardinal" borrows from the intellectual thinking of Amy Berkowitz, author of the 2015 collection *Tender Points*. Berkowitz' collection is where I came across the words of Elaine Scarry, author of the 1985 book *The Body in Pain: The Making and Unmaking of the World*, and the slogan of Socialist Patients' Collective. In "Cardinal" direct quotes from Scarry and Berkowitz are italicized.

6. "It used to be illegal for homosexuals to rest like this" references David Wojnarowicz's 1991 memoir *Close to the Knives : A Memoir of Disintegration*.

   The lines "every T-cell lost is ten pounds of rage" and "shoot the queers" reference the same passage.

   The passage reads: "'If you want to stop AIDS shoot the queers' says the governor of Texas on the radio and his press secretary later claims that the governor was only joking and didn't know the microphone was turned on and besides they didn't think it would hurt his chances for re-elections anyways. And I wake up every morning, and I wake up every morning in this killing machine called America. And I'm carrying this rage like a blood filled egg and there's a thin line between the inside and the outside, a thin line between thought and action and that line is simply made up of blood and muscle and bone and I'm waking up more and more from daydreams of tipping Amazonian blow darks in 'infected blood' and spitting them at the exposed necklines of certain politicians or government healthcare officials or those thinly disguised walking swastikas that wear religious garments over their murderous intentions or those rabid strangers parading against AIDS clinics in the nightly news suburbs. There's a thin line, a very thin line between the inside and outside and I've been looking all my life at the signs surrounding us in the media or on people's lips; the religious types outside St. Patrick's Cathedral shouting to men and women in the gay parade 'You won't be here next year—you'll get AIDS and die. Ha ha.' And the areas of the USA where it is possible to murder a man and when brought to trial one only has to say that the victim was a queer and that he tried to touch you and the courts will set you free. And the difficulties that a bunch of Republican Senators have in Albany with supporting an anti-violence bill that includes 'sexual orientation' as a category of crime victims. There's a thin line, a very thin line and as each T-cell disappears from my body it's replaced by ten pounds of pressure, ten pounds of rage, and I focus that rage into non-violent resistance, but the focus is starting to slip, the focus is starting to slip. My hands are beginning to move independent of self-restraint and the egg is starting to crack. America. America . . ." There is an audio clip of Wojnarowicz reading the full excerpt, available online from the Whitney Museum of Art.

7. "One Million Dead Men: An Empirical Investigation Into New Sodom" is peppered with factual historical references.

   The line "However, 85 percent of all those diagnosed with AIDS throughout the epidemic were between 20 and 49 . . ." is a real statistic, published by the Centers for Disease Control in a 2001 article titled "HIV and AIDS, United States, 1981—2000."

   The quote "landing a man on the moon and returning him safely to the Earth" was taken from former President John F. Kennedy's speech "Address to a Joint Session of Congress, May 25 1961."

8. "Blood Sister / Only Child" was influenced by Danez Smith's poem "summer, somewhere" from

their 2017 collection *Don't Call Us Dead.* I was specifically influenced by the section that begins with the lines "i loved a boy once & once he made me / a red dirge, skin casket, no burial."

9. "If you ask me why I read science fiction" was influenced by Franny Choi's 2017 poem "Introduction to Quantum Theory," published in *The Adroit Journal*.

Finally, there are a number of works and conversations that informed the emotion and spirit of the collection, rather than specific poems or lines.

I've had many formative interviews over the years as a journalist, but two have especially stayed with me. In 2018 I interviewed David Groff for *Lambda Literary Review*, and he spoke on literary executorship and the many artists and writers that fell (or were forced) into obscurity after dying from AIDS. From Groff, I began to understand that memory is like fire — it must be tended, constantly, by every generation.

Then in 2023 I interviewed Rev. Dr. Roland Stringfellow for *HuffPost*, where he spoke on angel actions—peaceful, protective counter-protests where people dressed as angels with huge wings so as to block, quite literally, anti-gay protestors and their pro-AIDS signs from view. The first angel action took place after the murder of Matthew Shepard and the practice has continued to the present, including memorial services for victims of the 2016 Pulse nightclub shooting. From Rev. Dr. Stringfellow, I began to reevaluate the possibilities and power of spirituality. I became more hopeful.

In no particular order, other influential works include:

So Many Stars: An Oral History of Trans, Nonbinary, Genderqueer and Two-Spirit People of Color by Caro De Robertis, specifically the chapter on the AIDS crisis; *13th Balloon* by Mark Bibbins; *Sojourners: Black Gay Voices in the Age of AIDS Volume II* published by Other Countries, specifically the many love letters and good-bye letters found within; *Borrowed Time: An Aids Memoir* by Paul Monette; *Up Against the Wall: Art, Activism, and the AIDS Poster* edited by Donald Albrecht, Jessica Lacher-Feldman and William M. Valenti; *the Fiasco: The AIDS Crisis* podcast from journalist Leon Neyfakh; The ACT UP Oral History Project; the 1990 film *Paris Is Burning* and the 2018 TV series *Pose*; the Brooklyn Museum exhibition *Copy Machine Manifestos: Artists Who Make Zines*, where I first saw copies of *Infected Faggot Perspectives* — and scribbled down this collection's opening epigraph.

Previous Publications

"Climate death but my blood runs hot" was originally published in *Queen Mob's Teahouse*, and again in my poetry chapbook *RUN.* from Finishing Line Press.

"Vertigo" was originally published by the *Broadkill Review*, where it was nominated for a Pushcart Prize in 2021.

"Salomé / Dark Blue" was originally published by *Ghost City Press* under the title "Medusa / Dark Blue."

An older version of "Blood shift" was originally published by *Cream City Review* as "NORTH FLORIDA CHOKES ME."

An older version of "Cardinal" was published by *Newfound Journal*, where it was nominated for Best New Voices in 2022.

Acknowledgments

Many hands played a part in shaping this collection.

Thank you first, and always, to my family.

Thank you to the many writers who lent their time, seriousness, and generosity to this story: my poet friends from Oxygente, with particular affection to Juan R. Palomo for reading this collection during an important moment; Marisa Lin, for being my companion on the page and off; and Rachel Komich, my first reader, last hope, and best friend.

Thank you to mentors and teachers who make the difference: Julie R. Enszer for ushering me into the brilliant, vibrant, and unending work of lesbian feminist thought and publishing; Vi Khi Nao, who worked with me on the very first draft those first few months of the pandemic. That collaboration gave *DEAD BOYS* its bones; David Baker and Victoria Chang from the Kenyon Poetry workshops; and Sarah Burke, who has supported me as a journalist, poet, and person.

Always, thank you to my wife, Salomé, who so generously lent her name to this collection and whose cover art said everything needed saying.

And, finally, thank you to the ghosts who live at the heart of this collection. I'm sorry you don't get to read it. I'm sorry I had reason to write it.

Also by YesYes Books

FICTION

The Nothing by Lauren Davis
Girls Like Me by Nina Packebush
Three Queerdos and a Baby by Nina Packebush
Book of Exemplary Women by Diana Xin

WRITING RESOURCES

Gathering Voices: Creating a Community-Based Poetry Workshop by Marty McConnell

FULL-LENGTH POETRY COLLECTIONS

Ugly Music by Diannely Antigua
Bone Language by Jamaica Baldwin
Cataloguing Pain by Allison Blevins
Strange Flowers by Bryan Byrdlong
What Runs Over by Kayleb Rae Candrilli
This, Sisyphus by Brandon Courtney
Salt Body Shimmer by Aricka Foreman
Gutter by Lauren Brazeal Garza
Forever War by Kate Gaskin
Inconsolable Objects by Nancy Miller Gomez
Ceremony of Sand by Rodney Gomez
Undoll by Tanya Grae
Loudest When Startled by luna rey hall
Everything Breaking / For Good by Matt Hart
Brine Orchid by Arah Ko
40 WEEKS by Julia Kolchinsky
murmurations by Anthony Thomas Lombardi
Sons of Achilles by Nabila Lovelace
Refusenik by Lynn Melnick

GOOD MORNING AMERICA I AM HUNGRY AND ON FIRE
by jamie mortara
Born Backwards by Tanya Olson
a falling knife has no handle by Emily O'Neill
To Love an Island by Ana Portnoy Brimmer
Another Way to Split Water by Alycia Pirmohamed
Tell This to the Universe by Katie Prince
One God at a Time by Meghan Privitello
I'm So Fine: A List of Famous Men & What I Had On
by Khadijah Queen
If the Future Is a Fetish by Sarah Sgro
Gilt by Raena Shirali
[insert] boy by Danez Smith
Say It Hurts by Lisa Summe
Hand Over Hand Over the Edge of the World by Patrick Swaney
Boat Burned by Kelly Grace Thomas
Helen Or My Hunger by Gale Marie Thompson
As She Appears by Shelley Wong

RECENT CHAPBOOK COLLECTIONS

Vinyl 45s

Exit Pastoral by Aidan Forster
Crown for the Girl Inside by Lisa Low
Phantasmagossip by Sara Mae
Year of the Sheep by Stacey Park
Scavenger by Jessica Lynn Suchon
Unmonstrous by John Allen Taylor
Giantess by Emily Vizzo

Blue Note Editions

Kissing Caskets by Mahogany L. Browne
One Above One Below: Positions & Lamentations by Gala Mukomolova
The Porch (As Sanctuary) by Jae Nichelle
The Only Way Out Is Through: Essays by Katie Jean Shinkle

www.ingramcontent.com/pod-product-compliance
Lightning Source LLC
LaVergne TN
LVHW052343100826
845147LV00021B/1172

9781946303134